#2

FRED VAN LENTE ★ RYAN DUNLAVEY

REAL HISTORY!
FAKE JOKES!

ABRAHAM
LINCOLN!

HARPER
alley

An Imprint of HarperCollinsPublishers

Harper Alley is an imprint of HarperCollins Publishers.

Library of Congress Control Number: 2017954078
ISBN 978-0-06-289121-1 (trade bdg.)
ISBN 978-0-06-289120-4 (pbk.)

The artist used Adobe Photoshop, a Wacom Cintiq tablet, and insomnia to create the digital illustrations for this book.

20 21 22 23 24 TC 10 9 8 7 6 5 4 3
❖
First Edition

For Gretchen, my super sis,
a great teacher and inspiration
—FVL

For Luke!
—RD

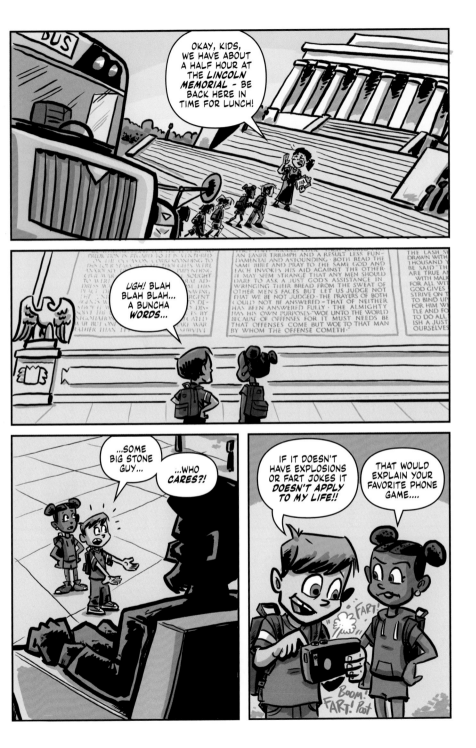

1

3

ABRAHAM LINCOLN WAS BORN IN 1809 INTO A COUNTRY *ALREADY* DIVIDED!

UNTIL THE *AMERICAN REVOLUTION*, SLAVERY EXISTED IN ALL *THIRTEEN* OF GREAT BRITAIN'S ORIGINAL COLONIES.

EUROPEANS BROUGHT ENSLAVED AFRICANS TO THE "NEW WORLD" TO DO THE WORK WHITE COLONISTS WOULDN'T DO — OR THERE SIMPLY WEREN'T ENOUGH WHITES *TO DO*.

BUT SLAVERY BECAME *MOST* IMPORTANT TO THE *SOUTHERN* PART OF THE COUNTRY. THE WARMER CLIMATE ALLOWED FOR *LARGE PLANTATIONS* GROWING RICE, TOBACCO, SUGAR, AND *COTTON*.

NORTH

NY
CT RI
PA
NJ
MD DE

SOUTH

VA
KY
NC
TN
SC
GA

These planters convinced themselves the only way to make a *profit* was if they used *slave labor*.

Slaves' lives were full of hardship and horror. They could be killed, abused, and sold away from their families for any reason. Under the law they were *property*, not people.

American slavery was inescapable. Anyone whose mother was a slave was *automatically* born a slave. It was nearly impossible for black slaves to buy or win their own freedom.

Northern states *began outlawing* slavery during and after the American Revolution, partly because it wasn't that important to their economy and violated the ideals of freedom for which so many Americans fought and died.

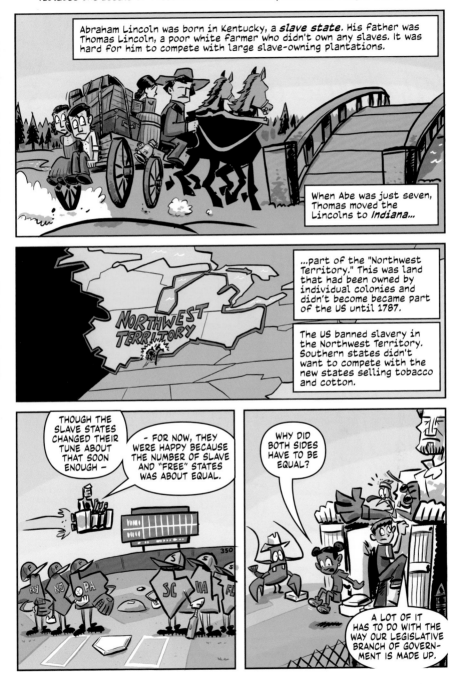

Abraham Lincoln was born in Kentucky, a *slave state*. His father was Thomas Lincoln, a poor white farmer who didn't own any slaves. It was hard for him to compete with large slave-owning plantations.

When Abe was just seven, Thomas moved the Lincolns to *Indiana*...

...part of the "Northwest Territory." This was land that had been owned by individual colonies and didn't become became part of the US until 1787.

The US banned slavery in the Northwest Territory. Southern states didn't want to compete with the new states selling tobacco and cotton.

THOUGH THE SLAVE STATES CHANGED THEIR TUNE ABOUT THAT SOON ENOUGH –

– FOR NOW, THEY WERE HAPPY BECAUSE THE NUMBER OF SLAVE AND "FREE" STATES WAS ABOUT EQUAL.

WHY DID BOTH SIDES HAVE TO BE EQUAL?

A LOT OF IT HAS TO DO WITH THE WAY OUR LEGISLATIVE BRANCH OF GOVERN-MENT IS MADE UP.

7

11

Sarah Bush brought **books** with her from Kentucky – and Abe discovered a love of **reading** he'd have for his whole life.

Among his favorites were his stepmother's Bible and her collection of **fables** from the Greek poet **Aesop**, including:

The FOUR OXEN & The LION by Aesop

Aesop (620-564 BCE) began life as a **slave** but became one of the most beloved authors of the ancients.

A lion used to prowl about a field in which Four Oxen used to dwell...

Many a time he tried to attack them; but whenever he came near they turned their tails to one another, so whichever way he approached them he was met by the horns of one of them.

At last however, they fell a-quarreling among themselves, and each went off to pasture alone in a separate corner of the field.

Then the Lion attacked them one by one and soon made an end of all four.

United we stand, divided we fall!

When he was president, Abraham Lincoln would say he always hated slavery.

"IF SLAVERY IS NOT WRONG, *NOTHING* IS WRONG!"

This attitude was no doubt helped by *Thomas* Lincoln, who would often hire his son out to neighboring farmers. Any money Abe made would go directly into Dad's pocket.

Abe would plow fields, pull pumpkins, and *split rails* for fences. And he wouldn't see a penny of the money he earned.

Obviously, Abe and his dad did not really get along. Perhaps he never forgave Thomas for leaving him and his sister alone in the forest.

And Thomas seemed to prefer his stepchildren and their mother to the kids from his *first* marriage.

Still, many of Thomas Lincoln's *better* qualities rubbed off on Abe. Tom never drank or smoke, and neither did Abe.

Tom was by all accounts an amazing *storyteller* and a great mimic, and Abe absorbed those qualities from him.

ONCE THERE WAS A COLLECTOR WHO WAS JUST *MAD* FOR OLD REVOLUTIONARY WAR STUFF....

When he was 21 years old, Abe helped his family move west again, to neighboring Illinois...

...then struck off on his own, arriving "like a piece of floating driftwood" (his words) to a village named New Salem.

NEW SALEM

He found a job as a cook on a flatboat delivering crops down the Mississippi River to New Orleans.

Abe became something of a celebrity shortly after the boat set off south.

THIS IS BAD.

Their boat got stuck on the dam of a nearby mill, and one end began filling up with water!

The quick-thinking Lincoln drilled a hole in the hanging end of the boat, draining the water....

Once he and the rest of the crew moved the cargo to the front of the boat...

YAAAAAAY!

SPPPSHHH

...he plugged the hole and they continued their journey south!

17

Later in life, Abe invented a means to keep boats afloat even in shallow water with "inflatable compartments" – like a balloon!

He remains the *only* US president ever to receive a government *patent* for an invention!

New Orleans was a massive *slave* metropolis, one of the main buying and selling places for human beings in the United States.

His crew later said the sight of human beings auctioned off in public upset him greatly.

The flatboat returned to New Salem with goods to sell in the local general store, which Abe helped run.

BERRY-LINCOLN

He was notoriously trustworthy, once walking three miles to track down a customer he had accidentally overcharged by *six and a half cents!*

BOY! YOU REALLY ARE *HONEST, ABE!*

Abe was well-suited to being a *shopkeeper.* Back then it was the main *gathering place* for townsfolk. He regaled his friends for hours on end with his jokes and stories, just as *Thomas* Lincoln once did.

ONCE THERE WAS A *MAN OF DARING,* QUICK-WITTED, SELF-POSSESSED, AND *EQUAL* TO ALL OCCASIONS...

...WHO WAS ASKED TO CARVE A *TURKEY* FOR A *LARGE PARTY.*

HEY!

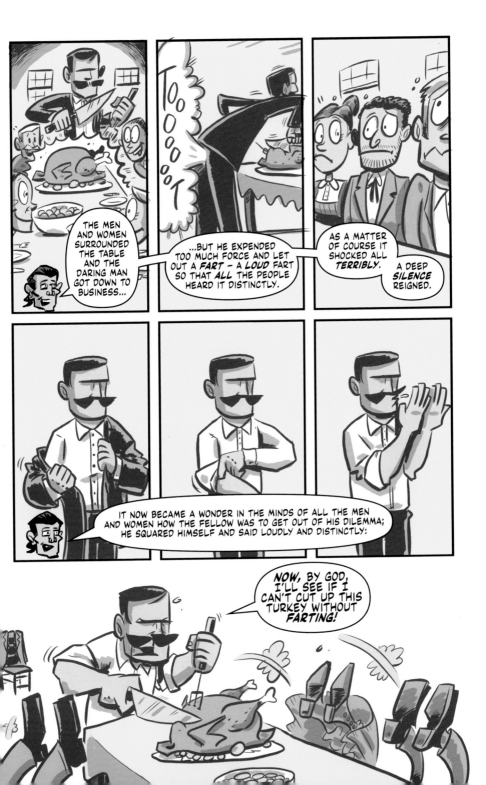

In 1832 the future war-time president got his first and only *military* experience when he joined the fight against the Sauk chief Black Hawk.

I WANT MY *LAND* BACK, AND YOU NAME A *HOCKEY TEAM* AFTER ME INSTEAD.

AMERICANS ARE WEIRD.

GO 'HAWKS!

Black Hawk had crossed the Mississippi into what was then Illinois (but is now Wisconsin) to reclaim Sauk lands lost in a disputed treaty.

Abe was popular enough in town that he was elected *captain* of the local militia.

He later joked he didn't see any fighting during the Black Hawk War — except against *mosquitoes*!

Once, when leading his men toward a fence, he realized he didn't remember the command to make them march *through* its gate.

UH...

He had to think of something quick!

...COMPANY DISMISSED!

FOR TWO MINUTES!

THEN FALL IN ON THE OTHER SIDE OF THE GATE!

⸫PHEW!⸫

Abe moved to the state capital, Springfield, in the center of the state, to begin his political career just as a major political *movement* in America was starting:

ABOLITIONISM

was a movement by free African Americans and their white allies to ban – or *abolish* – slavery in the United States.

ALL MEN ARE CREATED EQUAL

ONE OF THESE THINGS ...IS *NOT* LIKE THE OTHER...

Frederick Douglass (1818-1895), *another* great author born a slave!

Though Abraham Lincoln always hated slavery – he was not an abolitionist, and often said so.

100

0

-100

He was a *moderate* – someone taking *neither* side.

AYE!!

Still, a resolution saying abolitionists were *bad* passed the Illinois legislature by a vote of 77-6...and one of those no votes was Abraham Lincoln's.

Like many Americans, Abe believed if slavery weren't allowed to move *beyond* the South, people there would *tire* of it and it would basically die of *old age.*

IS SLAVERY DEAD YET?

NO! NOT YET!! SSSHH!

To abolitionists, Abe's attitude was a *fantasy* – slavery would continue to exist in America as long as America *allowed* it to.

Many Illinois settlers, like Abe, were born in the *South* and fiercely supported slavery. Despite being a *"free"* state, Illinois had *"Black Codes"* preventing African Americans from voting or holding political office.

On November 7, 1837, Rev. Elijah Lovejoy, a white minister who published an abolitionist newspaper in Alton, Illinois, was murdered by a mob and his printing press thrown in the river.

Lovejoy's murder horrified Abe, and he warned in an 1838 speech at Springfield's Young Men's Lyceum (sort of a speaker's club):

"SHALL WE EXPECT SOME TRANSATLANTIC MILITARY GIANT TO STEP THE OCEAN AND CRUSH US AT A BLOW? NEVER!

"AT WHAT POINT THEN IS THE APPROACH OF DANGER TO BE EXPECTED?"

"I ANSWER: IF IT EVER REACH US, IT MUST SPRING UP *AMONGST* US; IT CANNOT COME FROM ABROAD.

"IF DESTRUCTION BE OUR LOT, WE MUST *OURSELVES* BE ITS AUTHOR AND FINISHER."

Though he didn't say it at the time, Lincoln's point was clear:

"UNITED WE RISE, DIVIDED WE FALL."

Abe was getting to be known as a *speaker* beyond simply a teller of jokes. He loved *words* and crafted his speeches with incredible care.

These skills served him well in his *other* career. State lawmaker was not a *full-time job*. It didn't pay all that much.

Abe was also a traveling *lawyer*, going from town to town to help farmers on what was called the *"Mud Circuit."*

When he came to town, he looked like an *uneducated man* from the country — and that's just what Abe *wanted* people to think.

"Any man who took Lincoln for a *simple-minded man* would very soon wake up with his back in a *ditch*," said one lawyer who faced him.

I FIND FOR THE *DEFENSE!*

WHA'...WHA' HAPPENED?!?

Abe's secret weapon was his way with *words.*

He won the case of a Revolutionary War widow who had been robbed of her husband's army pension when he described the hardships of *Valley Forge* so dramatically, the jury was in *tears.*

WHEN HE RETURNED TO SPRINGFIELD TO MEET WITH THE REST OF THE LEGISLATURE, LINCOLN SAT WITH THE *WHIG* PARTY –

NO, RYAN! NOT *THAT* KIND OF WIG! WITH AN *"H"*!

OOPS – SORRY!

THEY WERE NAMED AFTER THE POLITICAL PARTY IN ENGLAND THAT OFTEN OPPOSED THE KING.

THE AMERICAN WHIGS ROSE TO OPPOSE DEMOCRATIC PRESIDENT *ANDREW JACKSON*, WHO HAD A FIERY TEMPER AND BOSSY STYLE THAT LED HIS ENEMIES TO CALL HIM "KING ANDREW."

I WANNA BE ON THE $20 BILL! JUST *'CAUSE!*

HE'S A KIIIIIIIIIIIING!!

The leader of the Democratic Party in Illinois was Stephen A. Douglas – short in size, big in ego, known as the *"Little Giant."*

YES. I KNOW.

I AM AWESOME.

HEY, MAN! GET OFF OUR *MOVIE SET!*

The pro-South Democrats were much more *popular* in Illinois than the Whigs, so Douglas was one of the most powerful politicians in the entire state.

In 1838, Abe went to a party in Springfield and saw the Little Giant talking up *Mary Todd*. Mary was a rich young woman who was living with relatives in town and was also from Abe's home state of Kentucky.

GULP!

WHAT ARE YOU SAYING? I CAN'T HEAR YOU FROM UP HERE!

25

I WANTED TO DANCE WITH YOU IN THE WORST WAY!

WELL, YOU CERTAINLY *ARE!*

Despite their clumsy first meeting, Abe and Mary both loved poetry and politics. Mary soon fell hard for the awkward lawyer and chose him over Douglas.

She became convinced that he could rise to the highest points in the land.

DOUGLAS IS "A VERY LITTLE, LITTLE GIANT BY THE SIDE OF MY TALL KENTUCKIAN..."

LOVE GOGGLES: ON

"...INTELLECTUALLY ABE TOWERS ABOVE DOUGLAS JUST AS HE DOES PHYSICALLY!"

To anyone not wearing love goggles, though, the ambitious Mary made the **wrong** choice of boyfriend.

LOVE GOGGLES: OFF

Stephen Douglas became one of the most *famous men* in America, first as Illinois Secretary of State, then as a judge, then as a United States senator!

While Abe remained where he **was** – a lawyer wandering the backcountry when he wasn't a humble state legislator.

Convinced he hadn't *done* enough in life to get married yet, he broke off his engagement to Mary.

OH, NO!

Abe once called women *"the only things that cannot hurt me that I am afraid of."*

Both fell into a deep depression for a year.

Finally, during the summer of 1842, Abe's close friend *Joshua Speed* was suffering his own doubts about his upcoming wedding.

I DON'T KNOW IF MARRIAGE IS RIGHT FOR ME!

AS LONG AS YOU LOVE YOUR LADY, WHAT ELSE CAN MATTER?

YOU MAKE A LOT OF GOOD POINTS, LINCOLN....

YEAH... I GUESS I DO!

Abe realized that he was also knocking down all of *his* worries about marrying Mary Todd!

They were reunited. Mary's father, however, didn't approve of their dating, so they met in secret in the parlor of Mary's friend.

HAVE YOU SEEN WHAT *JAMES SHIELDS* HAS DONE NOW?

OH, I *KNOW*! HE'S THE *WORST*!

James Shields was the *auditor* of Illinois, meaning he had the job of inspecting how the state spent money.

Shields had declared that Illinois would no longer accept its own paper money as payment for state taxes!

NOPE! *OUR* MONEY IS *NO GOOD* HERE!

WHA'?!?

Shields was a Democrat, and like his leader, "King Andrew," believed that *state banks* were just for the *rich* to make themselves richer.

I WOULDN'T MIND TAKING HIM *DOWN* A PEG.

HE'S SUCH A *DANDY!* THAT GIVES ME AN IDEA.

Soon letters began appearing in the local newspaper signed, "Aunt Becca." The letters made fun of how well Shields thought of himself:

"DEAR GIRLS, IT IS DISTRESSING, BUT I CANNOT MARRY YOU *ALL.*"

"IT IS NOT MY FAULT THAT I AM *SO* HANDSOME AND *SO* INTERESTING."

Shields didn't find this bullying at all funny.

WHO WROTE THIS REALLY?!

LINCOLN! ABE LINCOLN! NOT IN THE FACE!

LINCOLN, SHIELDS SAYS YOU'VE DAMAGED HIS HONOR! HE'S CHALLENGING YOU TO A *DUEL!*

A...A *WHAT* NOW?! REALLY? IN *1842?*

Dueling – formal **combat** between two people – was **illegal** in Illinois.

So duels were usually held on a small island in the Mississippi River between Illinois and Missouri...

...so many, in fact, it was known as...

BLOODY ISLAND

According to the traditional rules of dueling, the person **challenged** was able to decide a bunch of things, like **where** the duel was fought and what **weapons** could be used.

Abe chose to duel using **broadswords.**

He also said they had to face each other in a twelve-foot-deep **pit** divided by a wooden plank **neither** could cross.

12'

All this would take advantage of Abe's height (he was 6' 4", Shields only 5' 9"), and long arms, which the blade would make even longer.

YAWN!

Abe could hit Shields without his opponent being able even to **reach** him!

Lincoln hoped that stacking all the odds in his favor would force Shields to **back down** and call off the fight...but he was **wrong.**

People waiting on the riverbank were horrified to see a **body** sent back in a boat!

GAHHHHH! NO! THEY'LL HAVE TO TEAR DOWN THE LINCOLN MEMORIAL!!

OR BUILD ONE HERE?

One of Abe's friends noted that he'd never seen him look so *long* before making a joke, and began to believe Lincoln was *frightened*.

LET'S DO THIS.

UM, SERIOUSLY?

WAIT! WAIT! MY FRIENDS – THIS IS MADNESS!

SHIELDS, YOU AND LINCOLN HAVE WORKED TOGETHER BEFORE IN THE CAPITOL, EVEN THOUGH YOU'RE IN DIFFERENT PARTIES.

SURELY *SOME* COMPROMISE CAN BE WORKED OUT *WITHOUT* VIOLENCE!

WELL...IF *HE* ADMITS HE WROTE THE LETTERS, AND HE WAS *WRONG*...I GUESS MY HONOR WOULD BE *SATISFIED*.

I'M... I'M *SORRY*, SHIELDS. IT WAS ME...

...AND ME *ALONE*.

Abe didn't want his fiancée to face Shields's fury, so he left out *Mary's* part in the affair.

On shore, people discovered they'd been *pranked* by a friend of the duelists.

THAT'S NOT FUNNY!!

Abraham Lincoln and Mary Todd were married in a small ceremony in the Todd home on November 4, 1842.

They moved into their first (and only) house in Springfield in 1843. It's still there, and you can visit it today.

For Mary this was a *huge* change in lifestyle: she had grown up on a plantation in Kentucky where she had *slaves* to do all her housework.

Now she had to figure out how to do that more or less on her own. *Four boys* were born here: Robert, Eddie, Willie, and Tad.

The state legislators of the Whig Party took turns running for the House of Representatives seat in the Springfield area.

A "Hot Seat" ... get it?

If the Whig won, he went to Washington, DC, to serve for two years. In 1846 it was Abe's turn, and he beat his Democratic opponent.

He arrived in the House just as the United States defeated *Mexico* in a war that began when Mexico's former territory *Texas* joined the US.

¡¡NO ES BUENO!!

(Mexico's symbolic bird is an eagle too, from an old Aztec legend.)

Mexico claimed the USA started the war by attacking on *their* side of the Rio Grande.

¡AQUI!

HERE!

But US president *James K. Polk* claimed Mexico had attacked the US.

One of Abe's first acts in Congress was to demand that the president prove which country started the war and *where*.

POLK MUST SHOW US THE EXACT *SPOT!*

?!?!?

As you might guess, siding with America's *enemy* in a war is not the most popular thing for an American politician to do.

The White House just *ignored* Abe, and the other congressmen made fun of him *mercilessly*, naming him *"Spotty"* Lincoln!

AS NICKNAMES GO, I LIKED "HONEST ABE" WAY BETTER.

First Capitol Dome (it was green!)

Abe's other major cause in Congress ended in *failure*, too. He was unable to get enough votes to *ban the slave trade* in Washington, DC.

AND RIGHT OVER *HERE* YOU CAN SEE THE LAND OF THE *FREE*....

ONE OF THESE THINGS IS NOT LIKE THE OTHER....

A major slave auction site was just *seven blocks* from the United States Capitol!

When Abe handed off his congressional seat to the next Whig, that guy was defeated by a Mexican War veteran.

BEAT IT, CHUMP!

Many Whigs blamed Abe's unpopular *antiwar* stand for their defeat.

Still, on this issue and DC slavery, Abe took comfort that he had been *defeated* doing the *right* thing.

I'M NOT SAYING THE MEXICAN WAR WAS *ONLY* ABOUT GRABBING NEW LANDS...

...BUT IT REMINDS ME OF THE FARMER WHO ONCE SAID:

"I AIN'T GREEDY 'BOUT *LAND*. I ONLY WANTS *WHAT JOINS MINE!*"

MINE

Abe returned to his Springfield law practice in 1849, convinced his career in politics was *over*.

33

In the peace treaty, Mexico gave up a *lot* of "what joins mine."

¡NO ES BUENO!

The US gained what's now the states of New Mexico, Arizona, California, Nevada, Utah, *and* parts of Wyoming and Colorado!

This, of course, *immediately* restarted the argument as to whether the new states would be *free* or have *slavery*.

TEXAS WILL BE A SLAVE STATE!

AND CALIFORNIA WILL BE FREE!

WHAT ABOUT US?

Utah and *New Mexico*, largely *desert*, were useless for the large plantations that used slave labor.

THE *FREE* STATES SHOULD TAKE BOTH!

NO WAY, THE *SLAVE* STATES SHOULD!

But the slave states were increasingly alarmed by the larger population and industrial power of their northern neighbors. They wanted to add as much territory to their "side" as possible.

HOLD ON HERE! *I'VE* GOT AN IDEA.

LOOK, EVERYBODY! IT'S US SENATOR FROM ILLINOIS *STEPHEN A. DOUGLAS!*

WHEN THERE ARE ENOUGH PEOPLE IN EACH STATE, THEY CAN *VOTE* ON WHETHER THEY SHOULD BE SLAVE OR FREE!

LET THE *CITIZENS* DECIDE!

Then, in 1854, the US had to carve out two *new* western states, Kansas and Nebraska. Both were north of the Missouri Compromise line, so they should have automatically been *free* states, but...

Now that free and slave states had to compete with each other for territory, the relationship between North and South **worsened**...

...but it was about to get **worsener**.

The United States Constitution divides the government into three **coequal** branches:

Congress, the legislative branch, **passes** laws...

...the executive branch, headed by the president, **enforces** laws...

...and the nine justices of the **Supreme Court** decide if laws obey the **Constitution**.

Dred Scott was born a slave in Virginia. In 1846, after failing to buy his family's freedom, he sued his master's widow, or challenged her in court.

Scott argued that since his master had taken him to the **free states** of Illinois and Wisconsin to live, it was **illegal** to keep him enslaved.

In the American court system, if you **lose** at one level, you can **appeal**, or ask again, to a higher and higher court –

– until you finally reach the **Supreme** Court, which is the **final** decider of what is and is not constitutional.

The whole situation disgusted Abraham Lincoln. He wrote a friend:

The candidates agreed to a specific format for the debates:

One man spoke for one hour, the next replied for ninety minutes, then the first was allowed to wrap up for thirty minutes.

Then, in the next town, whoever went first last time went second, and so on for seven debates – over *100,000 miles* of Illinois territory!

Douglas used a couple tactics against Abe:

I HAVE KNOWN MR. LINCOLN FOR NEARLY *TWENTY-FIVE* YEARS – HE COULD BEAT ANY OF THE BOYS WRESTLING OR RUNNING A FOOT RACE –

– HE COULD RUIN MORE *LIQUOR* THAN ALL THE BOYS OF THE TOWN TOGETHER!

LIE.

First, he made Abe sound like the ignorant *hayseed* his own jokes made him out to be.

Of course, that could *backfire.*

YOU KNOW, JUDGE DOUGLAS'S STAND ON SLAVERY REMINDS ME OF A CERTAIN *MAN OF DARING*...

...WHO WAS ASKED TO CARVE A *TURKEY* FOR A *LARGE PARTY*...

Later, Douglas would remember:

"EVERY ONE OF HIS STORIES SEEMS LIKE A *WHACK UPON MY BACK*.... NOTHING ELSE – NOT ANY OF HIS *ARGUMENTS* OR ANY OF HIS REPLIES TO MY QUESTIONS – DISTURBS ME.

"BUT WHEN HE BEGINS TO TELL A *STORY*, I FEEL THAT I AM TO BE *OVER-MATCHED*!"

...WITHOUT *FARTING!*

HA HA

HA HA

43

I SAY IT IS *BECAUSE* THEY WANTED SLAVERY TO *DIE OUT* IN TIME!

THEY KNEW – AS *I* DO – THERE IS A *CONTRADICTION* BETWEEN THE IDEALS AND MORALS ON WHICH THIS COUNTRY WAS FOUNDED AND THE PRINCIPLE OF *SLAVERY* –

– WHICH IS "*YOU* WORK AND TOIL AND EARN BREAD...AND *I'LL* EAT IT!"

CLAP CLAP CLAP CLAP CLAP CLAP CLAP

Today *we the people* directly elect United States senators. But in Lincoln's day, *state legislators* voted on who to send to Washington.

As Douglas and Lincoln crisscrossed the state debating, they were really campaigning *not* for themselves but for the men who would go to Springfield and elect *them.*

Lincoln did very well in the debates, and people were impressed by him. But in the end the *Democratic Party* still held the stronger position in Illinois.

ALL THE VOTES ARE *IN*, ABE....

THE DEMOCRATS HAVE A CLEAR *MAJORITY* IN SPRINGFIELD. THEY'LL SEND *DOUGLAS* TO THE SENATE, NOT YOU.

AH, WELL. SO IT GOES....

BUT MORE PEOPLE *VOTED* FOR THE REPUBLICANS THAN THE DEMOCRATS – SO YOU KNOW YOUR IDEAS ARE *MORE POPULAR!*

THAT *IS* GOOD NEWS – THANKS!

45

46

As a result, Lincoln was considered a serious Republican candidate for *president* in the next election!

Cooper Union, a free school in New York City, invited him to speak on any topic he liked.

Lincoln leaped at the opportunity to take the stage in the biggest and richest city in the country.

THE SLAVEHOLDING STATES ARE ALREADY THREATENING TO *LEAVE* THE UNION IF A REPUBLICAN LIKE MYSELF IS ELECTED PRESIDENT!

AND THEY CLAIM IT WILL BE *OUR* FAULT THAT IT HAPPENS!

THAT'S LIKE A HIGHWAYMAN HOLDING A PISTOL TO MY EAR, MUTTERING THROUGH HIS TEETH:

GIVE ME YOUR MONEY, OR I SHALL *KILL* YOU...

...AND THEN *YOU* WILL BE A MURDERER!

The big-city folk were as impressed with Abe as the prairie folk were.

The Republicans held a nominating convention in *Chicago* in Abe's home state of Illinois to decide their candidate for the 1860 election.

"Wigwam" = nickname for Republicans' convention center

47

It was considered *bad taste* for a candidate to appear at the nominating convention. Abe waited for the results from Chicago in a vacant lot in Springfield, where he played handball and told *stories*.

IT APPEARS THAT SHORTLY AFTER THE REVOLUTION WAS WON, *GENERAL ALLEN* HAD REASON TO *VISIT* ENGLAND...

Gen. ETHAN ALLEN (1738-1789), American Revolutionary War hero, cofounder of Vermont

...AND WHILE HE WAS THERE THE ENGLISH TOOK GREAT PLEASURE IN *TEASING* HIM.

ONE DAY THEY GOT A PICTURE OF GENERAL WASHINGTON, AND HUNG IT UP IN THE *OUTHOUSE* WHERE MR. ALLEN COULD SEE IT.

MR. ALLEN, DID YOU SEE THAT PICTURE OF YOUR FRIEND IN THE OUTHOUSE?

I THINK THAT A VERY GOOD PLACE FOR AN ENGLISHMAN TO KEEP IT.

WHY?

During the campaign, *Grace Bedell*, an eleven-year-old girl from New York state, wrote to Lincoln and advised him to grow a *beard* so he'd look a bit more attractive.

"THE LADIES LIKE *WHISKERS* AND THEY WOULD TEASE THEIR *HUSBANDS* TO VOTE FOR YOU."

It wasn't until 1920 that women were granted the right to vote in the US.

Even though many southern states didn't even bother putting Abe *on* the ballot, he *still* won the most votes!

LINCOLN 39%
DOUGLAS 29%
BELL 12%
BRECKENRIDGE 18%

Abe thought this sound advice and grew the beard he's famous for today.

Abraham Lincoln was going to be the sixteenth president of the United States – and *millions of people* were none too happy about that!

THAT *DOES* IT – I'M *OUTTA* HERE!

SC

On November 9, 1860, South Carolina voted to *secede* from the rest of the United States!

se·ces·sion (suh-sesh-shun) is the act of leaving a political state (like, you know, a *Union* of united states).

States had been threatening to secede since the first days of the USA, but no one had ever actually *tried* it before.

MASSACHUSETTS IS UP TO OUR EYEBALLS IN DEBT! WE WILL *SECEDE* IF YOU DON'T DO THIS PLAN!

WELL, MAYBE *WE'LL* SECEDE IF THEY *DO!* NYAH!

(previously on *Action Presidents: George Washington!*)

South Carolina argued that the states were "sovereign," meaning they really ruled themselves, because they preexisted the Union...so they could leave whenever they wanted!

DOINK!

By January 1861, five more southern states followed South Carolina's lead: Mississippi, Florida, Alabama, Georgia, and Louisiana.

THE NEXT MONTH, TEXAS ALSO JOINED WHAT BECAME KNOWN AS THE *CONFEDERATE STATES OF AMERICA* —

THAT MEANS IT'S PAPPY'S TIME TO SHINE!

WHAT ARE YOU — ERRKK!

I HEREBY DECLARE I AM SECEDING FROM THIS COMIC BOOK!

ACTION PRESIDENTS

JEFFERSON DAVIS

52

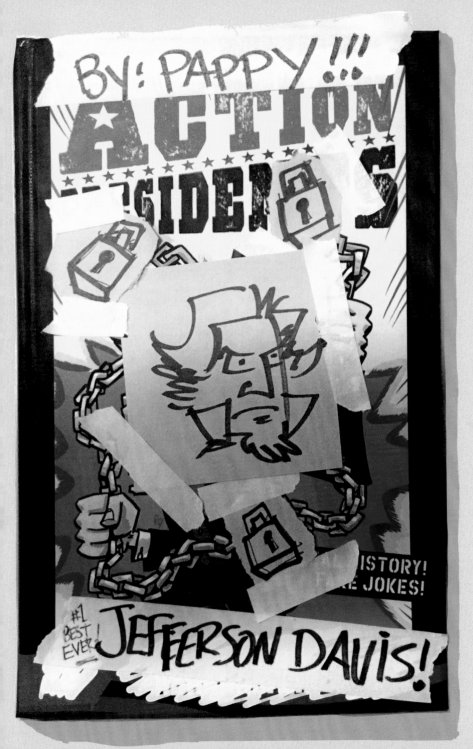

Some people wanted to make sure Lincoln *never* saw his adopted hometown again.

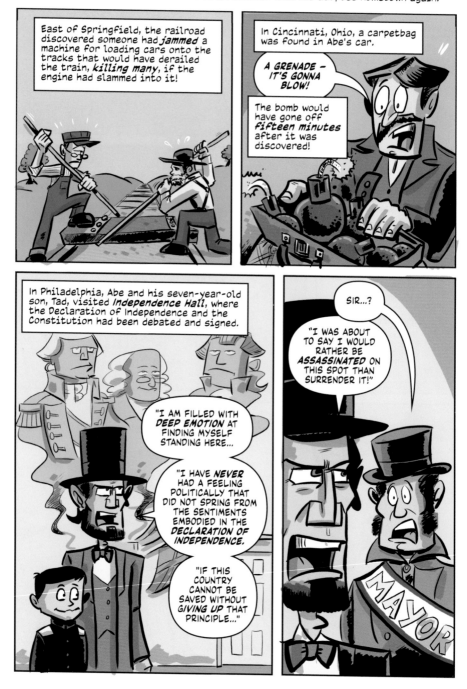

East of Springfield, the railroad discovered someone had *jammed* a machine for loading cars onto the tracks that would have derailed the train, *killing many,* if the engine had slammed into it!

In Cincinnati, Ohio, a carpetbag was found in Abe's car.

A GRENADE — IT'S GONNA BLOW!

The bomb would have gone off *fifteen minutes* after it was discovered!

In Philadelphia, Abe and his seven-year-old son, Tad, visited *Independence Hall,* where the Declaration of Independence and the Constitution had been debated and signed.

"I AM FILLED WITH *DEEP EMOTION* AT FINDING MYSELF STANDING HERE...

"I HAVE *NEVER* HAD A FEELING POLITICALLY THAT DID NOT SPRING FROM THE SENTIMENTS EMBODIED IN THE *DECLARATION OF INDEPENDENCE.*

"IF THIS COUNTRY CANNOT BE SAVED WITHOUT *GIVING UP* THAT PRINCIPLE..."

SIR...?

"I WAS ABOUT TO SAY I WOULD RATHER BE *ASSASSINATED* ON THIS SPOT THAN SURRENDER IT!"

MAYOR

The danger wasn't over when Abe went to give his *inaugural address.* Army sharpshooters surrounded the unfinished Capitol dome with orders that if anyone disrupted the speech, they should...

"BLOW THEM TO HELL!"

General Winfield "Old Fuss and Feathers" Scott (1786-1866)

As Abe mounted the podium to address the massive crowd of tens of thousands, he realized there was no place to set aside his hat and cane.

?!

Seated nearby, Abe's former nemesis *Stephen A. Douglas* offered to hold them during the speech.

NO HARD FEELINGS! WE'RE ALL IN THIS *TOGETHER* NOW!

"FELLOW-CITIZENS OF THE *UNITED* STATES..."

He really emphasized the "United" part!

IN HIS *FIRST INAUGURAL ADDRESS,* ABE DID A BUNCH OF IMPORTANT THINGS.

YAY!

He *reminded* the South he had repeatedly said he wasn't going to take away *their* slaves.

I WUV YOU. MWAH MWAH MWAH

not the real Abe

Of course, that wasn't *good enough* for slaveholders — they demanded a president who *loved* slavery!

But the most important thing he said was:

"I HOLD THAT IN CONTEMPLATION OF *UNIVERSAL LAW* AND OF THE CONSTITUTION, THE UNION OF THESE STATES IS *PERPETUAL*."

Meaning secession by its very nature was *illegal*!

A government could never *permit* secession. It's a built-in self-destruct mechanism like for a mad scientist's laboratory in a bad movie.

GO BOOM

FOOLS!! THE SECRETS OF *DEMOCRACY* DIE WITH *ME*!!

Almost *all* states went straight from being British colonies (or US territories) to being members of the Union. There was no *in-between* state for them to return *to*.

NOOOOOOO! I AM FALLING INTO A VAST UNCHARTED VOID!!

As president, he had to make sure that the laws of the Union were faithfully executed in *all* the States.

After the ceremony, the *outgoing* president, James Buchanan, dropped the Lincolns off at the White House.

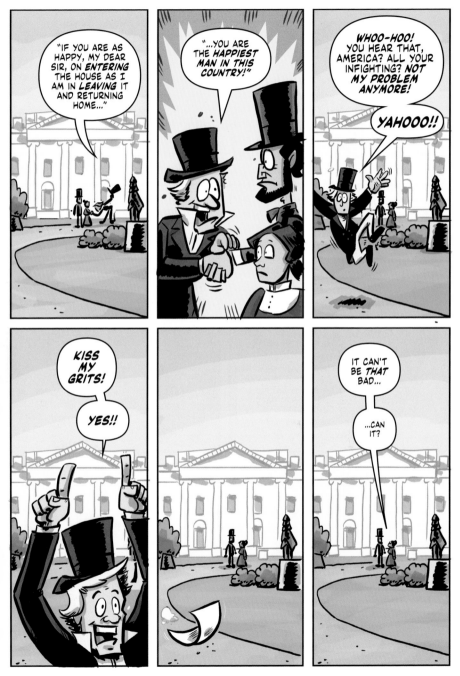

The Lincolns were horrified to discover that the White House, neglected for years, looked, in the words of Abe's secretary, like "an old and unsuccessful hotel."

GAAAHH!

(Soon Mary would launch a campaign to save it.)

In his speech Abe promised to maintain and hold forts, built and owned by the Federal government, now on Confederate soil...

...like Fort Sumter, on a tiny island in Charleston Harbor, South Carolina.

1st flag of CSA (in use Mar. 4, 1861 – May 1863)

Thousands of Confederate troops surrounded Sumter and the dozens of Union soldiers inside and demanded it be turned over to the CSA –

HEY! YOU'RE IN A DIFFERENT COUNTRY NOW! WE CALL DIBS!

NO WAY! WE HAVE TRIPLE-SUPER-ETERNAL DIBS!

CSA Gen. P.G.T. Beauregard (1818–1893), "The Man with Too Many Initials"

– at the same time the Lincolns were moving into the White House!

WELL, HOPEFULLY MY INAUGURAL ADDRESS WILL HELP THE SOUTH UNDER-STAND *WAR* IS NOT THE ANSWER....

The room that Abe used for his office was turned into the "Lincoln Bedroom" in today's White House!

MESSAGE FROM FORT SUMTER, SIR! THE REBELS HAVE THEM CUT OFF!

ARGH.

(This was literally the *first thing* that happened when Abe walked into his office!)

64

In April 1861 Abe decided to send only *food* to the trapped soldiers, making good on his promise that the North would not fire a *first shot.*

THAT'S OKAY! *WE* WILL!

The rebels opened fire on Fort Sumter on April 12.

The fort held out as long as it could, but the Union forces were hopelessly outmanned and outgunned.

HMM — *FASTBALL* MISSED! LET'S GO FOR A *SLIDER!*

WHAT IS HE *TALKING* ABOUT?

Capt. Abner Doubleday (1819-1893), "inventor" of baseball, fired 1st return shot at Fort Sumter

With many of the fort's buildings *on fire,* the commander surrendered to the CSA on the afternoon of the next day.

The first shots of the Civil War had been fired —

— along with the first *killed-in-action* on either side — in both cases by cannons that *misfired,* killing a Confederate and a Union man each!

BOOM

BOOM

BOOM

BOOM

BOOM

BOOM

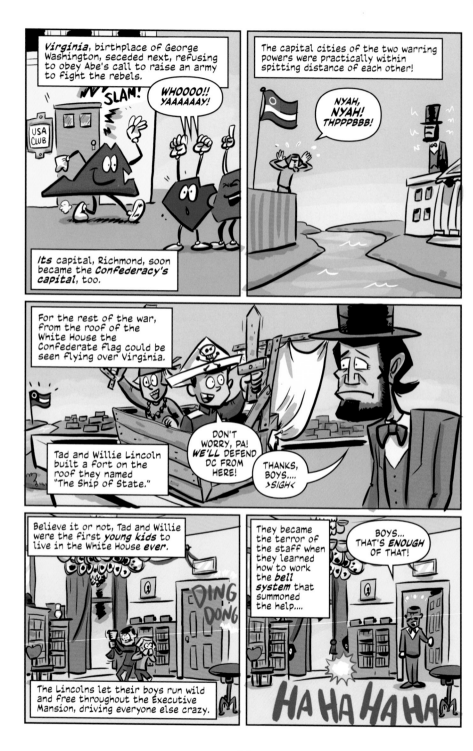

Virginia, birthplace of George Washington, seceded next, refusing to obey Abe's call to raise an army to fight the rebels.

WHOOOO!! YAAAAAAY!

SLAM!

USA CLUB

Its capital, Richmond, soon became the *Confederacy's capital*, too.

The capital cities of the two warring powers were practically within spitting distance of each other!

NYAH, NYAH! THPPPBBB!

For the rest of the war, from the roof of the White House the Confederate flag could be seen flying over Virginia.

DON'T WORRY, PA! *WE'LL* DEFEND DC FROM HERE!

THANKS, BOYS.... >SIGH<

Tad and Willie Lincoln built a fort on the roof they named "The Ship of State."

Believe it or not, Tad and Willie were the first *young kids* to live in the White House *ever*.

DING DONG

The Lincolns let their boys run wild and free throughout the Executive Mansion, driving everyone else crazy.

They became the terror of the staff when they learned how to work the *bell system* that summoned the help....

BOYS... THAT'S *ENOUGH* OF THAT!

HA HA HA HA

They loved to wrestle Abe to the ground with their friends — and he loved to fight them off!

JULIE, COME QUICK — SIT ON HIS STOMACH!

Julia Taft, 16, sister to the boys' friends, their unofficial babysitter

Despite the president telling her she didn't have to, Julia Taft couldn't help standing up every time he walked into the room.

JULIE, I WISH YOU'D STOP DOING THAT....

SIR YES SIR!

LISTEN, WILLIE, I WROTE A POEM ABOUT THE WAR:

"Old Abe Lincoln A RAIL-SPLITTER was he, and that's the way he'll split the CONFEDERACY."

TAD, THAT'S DISRESPECTFUL.

I DON'T CARE. EVERYONE KNOWS PA USED TO SPLIT RAILS.

69

A lot of government jobs were open because they had been held by Southerners who left Washington to serve the Confederacy.

YOU'RE MY *BROTHER-IN-LAW*, BEN, BUT YOU'RE ALSO A GRADUATE OF WEST POINT, HOW'D YOU LIKE TO BE *PAYMASTER* IN THE UNION ARMY??

THAT... THAT'S GENEROUS OF YOU, ABE — ER, *MR. PRESIDENT.*

Benjamin Hardin Helm (1831-1863), married to Mary Todd's half sister

BUT...OUR HOME STATE, KENTUCKY, IS A *SLAVE* STATE...AND EVEN THOUGH IT'S STAYED LOYAL TO THE UNION...I DON'T KNOW IF I CAN FIGHT *AGAINST* SLAVERY....

IT WOULD MEAN A *LOT* TO ME TO HAVE YOU FIGHT BY MY SIDE, BEN....

WE'RE FAMILY!

LET... LET ME THINK ABOUT IT....

As Helm agonized over what to do, he ran into a friend of his, another West Pointer, *Colonel Robert E. Lee.*

Washington Monument, under construction (opens 1888)

WHAT'S BOTHERING YOU, BEN?

THE PRESIDENT OFFERED ME A MAJOR POST IN THE MILITARY.... BUT...

70

THE NORTHERN STRATEGY

played to the region's **strengths.**

The North had more factories, so it could make more **guns.** It had more **railroads** to get troops to battlefields more quickly.

And even more important, the North had more **free people.**

Their numbers could be replaced by **immigrants** from other countries who had come to the North for jobs that weren't available in the slave labor-fueled South.

Wars are often decided by who can **outlast** the other side.

Old "Fuss and Feathers" Scott developed the North's first plan for victory. He called it "**The Anaconda Plan,**" because the North would circle the South like a snake.

First, they'd blockade Southern ports with the Union Navy. Then they'd seize the **Mississippi River,** which would **cut** the Confederacy in two.

From these two extremes the Union would push in, strangling the rebels like a great serpent.

URRKK!

THE SOUTHERN STRATEGY

played to what they saw as their strengths, too.

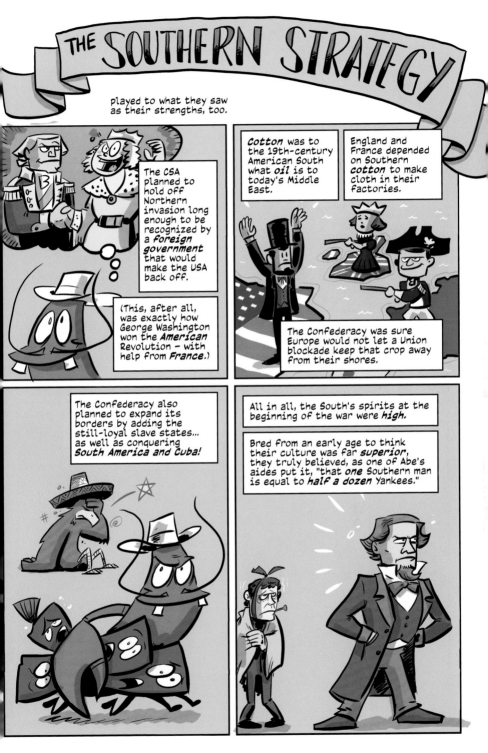

The CSA planned to hold off Northern invasion long enough to be recognized by a **foreign government** that would make the USA back off.

(This, after all, was exactly how George Washington won the **American Revolution** – with help from **France**.)

Cotton was to the 19th-century American South what **oil** is to today's Middle East.

England and France depended on Southern **cotton** to make cloth in their factories.

The Confederacy was sure Europe would not let a Union blockade keep that crop away from their shores.

The Confederacy also planned to expand its borders by adding the still-loyal slave states... as well as conquering **South America and Cuba!**

All in all, the South's spirits at the beginning of the war were **high.**

Bred from an early age to think their culture was far **superior**, they truly believed, as one of Abe's aides put it, "that **one** Southern man is equal to **half a dozen** Yankees."

73

The South seemed to prove their superiority, too, after Fort Sumter, when the Northern public demanded Lincoln *strike* against the rebels *immediately.*

On July 21, 1861, Union troops marched on Richmond across the *Bull Run* stream.

Washington's elite people were so sure that they were about to achieve an easy and *final* victory that they gathered to watch the battle like it was an outdoor concert.

But the Union men were beaten back by a strong Confederate counterattack.

The North's hopes of a quick end to the war were swiftly dashed.

Still, Abe knew his history. He remembered George Washington's many early struggles during the Revolution.

He thought there would most likely be a long war ahead – and he made sure his generals knew to drill their soldiers to be ready for it.

"Old Fuss and Feathers" Winfield Scott was forced into retirement after the defeat at Bull Run, taking the fall for a battle he wasn't even *at.*

He was replaced by *George McClellan,* a young general with a royal bearing who was known as "*Young Napoleon.*"

He had a pretty *high* opinion of himself and believed the war and the country would be much better off if he was made *dictator*.

He agreed with Abe on the need for more training of the men, but he trained his men *so* well that he seemed reluctant to actually use them in *battle*.

ARE YOU ATTACKING TODAY?

NO! I NEED MORE TROOPS!

TODAY?

NO! WEATHER'S BAD!

DARE I HOPE? TODA—

LOOK HOW MANY *CANNONS* THE REBELS HAVE!

MY BEAUTIFUL ARMY MIGHT GET *HURT!!*

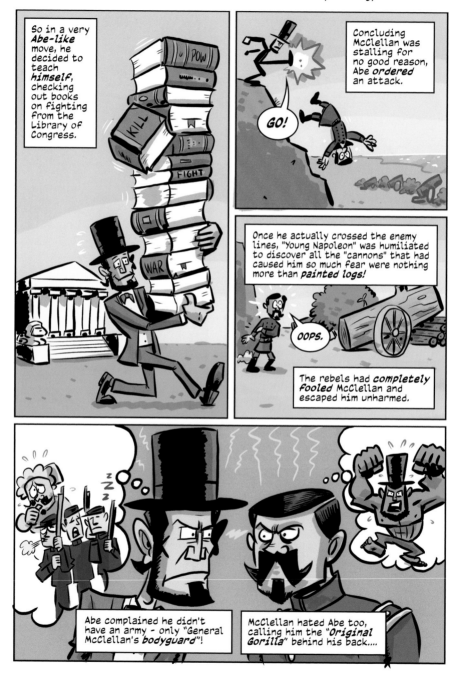

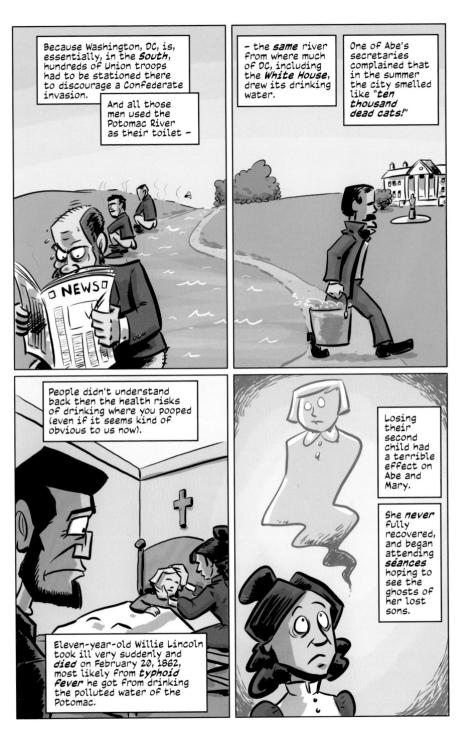

Because Washington, DC, is, essentially, in the *South*, hundreds of Union troops had to be stationed there to discourage a Confederate invasion.

And all those men used the Potomac River as their toilet –

– the *same* river from where much of DC, including the *White House*, drew its drinking water.

One of Abe's secretaries complained that in the summer the city smelled like "*ten thousand dead cats!*"

People didn't understand back then the health risks of drinking where you pooped (even if it seems kind of obvious to us now).

Eleven-year-old Willie Lincoln took ill very suddenly and *died* on February 20, 1862, most likely from *typhoid fever* he got from drinking the polluted water of the Potomac.

Losing their second child had a terrible effect on Abe and Mary.

She *never* fully recovered, and began attending *séances* hoping to see the ghosts of her lost sons.

In addition to his *personal* tragedy, the president also had to deal with the fact that the war was going *badly* for the North.

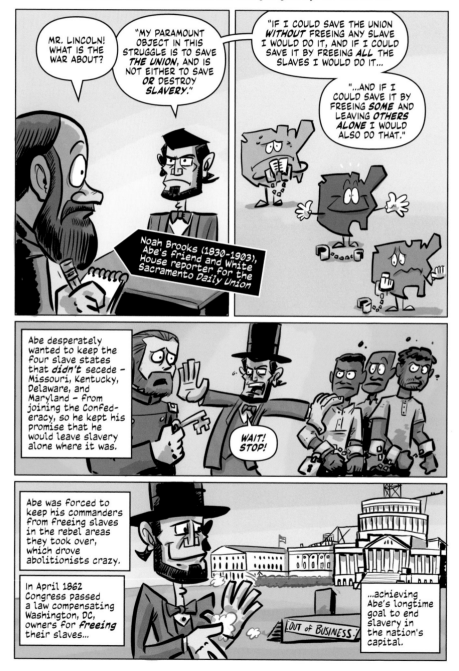

MR. LINCOLN! WHAT IS THE WAR ABOUT?

"MY PARAMOUNT OBJECT IN THIS STRUGGLE IS TO SAVE *THE UNION*, AND IS NOT EITHER TO SAVE *OR* DESTROY *SLAVERY*."

"IF I COULD SAVE THE UNION *WITHOUT* FREEING ANY SLAVE I WOULD DO IT, AND IF I COULD SAVE IT BY FREEING *ALL* THE SLAVES I WOULD DO IT...

"...AND IF I COULD SAVE IT BY FREEING *SOME* AND LEAVING *OTHERS ALONE* I WOULD ALSO DO THAT."

Noah Brooks (1830-1903), Abe's friend and White House reporter for the Sacramento *Daily Union*

Abe desperately wanted to keep the four slave states that *didn't* secede – Missouri, Kentucky, Delaware, and Maryland – from joining the Confederacy, so he kept his promise that he would leave slavery alone where it was.

WAIT! STOP!

Abe was forced to keep his commanders from freeing slaves in the rebel areas they took over, which drove abolitionists crazy.

In April 1862 Congress passed a law compensating Washington, DC, owners for *freeing* their slaves...

OUT of BUSINESS

...achieving Abe's longtime goal to end slavery in the nation's capital.

78

Then, on July 22, 1862, Abe read to his cabinet the first draft of something he called the "Emancipation Proclamation."

It declared that all the slaves in the Confederate states were free men and women starting on the first day of 1863.

The proclamation wasn't just the right thing to do, it was also smart military strategy.

Slaves worked in factories making Confederate weapons, in Confederate hospitals as nurses and cooks, and as builders of Confederate forts. Abe wanted to rob the South of all that free labor!

NURSE...*KOF!* MY BEDPAN NEEDS CHANGING! NURSE?

Also, the powers of Europe, which had abolished slavery years ago, would not support the proslavery side of a Civil War.

BUT – BUT I THOUGHT YOU *LIKED* ME!

GOTCHA!

Lincoln believed he had no legal authority to end slavery in the *Union* – but in the states under *rebellion* he could end it under the *war powers* granted the president by the Constitution.

What exactly would *happen* to the freed slaves was another question entirely.

– and his advisers said he must *wait* for a *Union victory* to announce it. Otherwise the government would look *desperate.*

Robert E. Lee gave him his chance when the Confederate army marched into still-loyal Maryland on September 3, 1862.

"SHE IS NOT DEAD, NOR DEAF, NOR DUMB – HUZZA! SHE SPURNS *THE NORTHERN SCUM!* SHE BREATHES! SHE BURNS! SHE'LL COME! SHE'LL COME! *MARYLAND! MY MARYLAND!*"

"Maryland, My Maryland" (1861) is *still* the official state song of Maryland even with those anti-Union lyrics!

Lee thought Marylanders would greet his men as fellow slavery-loving heroes – *instead* they cheered when Little Mac's Union troops arrived!

Incredibly, two Union sergeants discovered Lee's *battle plans* wrapped around *three cigars!*

TOP SECRET.

McClellan caught up with Lee at *Antietam Creek* on September 17, 1862, in one of the *bloodiest battles* in human history.

Men still fought in neat rows like they had for centuries, lining, shooting, reloading, and shooting again.

In the end, McClellan won, and Abe had his *victory*. He announced he was going to *sign* the Emancipation Proclamation on *New Year's Day*, 1863.

Predictably, the Confederacy *freaked out.*

A Union private wrote, "There is nothing [the Rebels] seem to feel so much, and care so much about, as to *lose their slaves*. I honestly believe that many of them would rather have us *kidnap their children...*"

TAKE PAPPIA AND PAPPY JUNIOR INSTEAD! *PLEASE!!*

In the North, not everybody loved the Emancipation Proclamation. Racist whites like Abe's own commander, George McClellan, *hated* it. He called it:

"AN *ACCURSED* DOCTRINE..."

"YOU WILL SAY YOU WILL NOT FIGHT TO *FREE NEGROES*.

"*SOME* OF THEM SEEM *WILLING* TO FIGHT FOR *YOU*..."

The Proclamation also allowed African Americans to join the *army* and risk their lives in *battle*.

But the Confederate Congress also passed a law that any black troops would be *enslaved* or *shot*, and any *white* Union officer captured commanding black troops would be *executed*.

The annual New Year's Day party at the White House was exceptionally *happy* in 1863. Abe and Mary shook hands with the public for two hours straight.

Around noon, Abe felt blisters forming on his hand.

He excused himself and went up to his office to meet his Secretary of State, William Seward, and his son and assistant Frederick.

Secretary of State = US Chief *Diplomat*

The Sewards spread the Proclamation out across a table before the fire.

A Proclamation

"I NEVER IN MY LIFE FELT MORE CERTAIN I WAS DOING *RIGHT*, THAN I DO IN SIGNING THIS PAPER."

But *nothing* changed for slaves at *first*.
Until the Confederacy was defeated, the Emancipation could
not be *enforced*. On the battlefield, fighting *dragged on.*

At *home*, Abe found he was a target too. Once, riding through the woods:

BANG!

WHOA, BOY, CAREFUL — JUST A STRAY GUNSHOT!

But, once he got home:

YOU'RE LUCKY YOU WEAR SUCH A TALL HAT, PA!

GULP! NOT SO "STRAY" AFTER ALL!

He never rode anywhere without an escort after that.

But that didn't stop killers from trying to get to him.

On July 2, 1863, Abe and Mary were returning to the White House from their country home.

No one noticed someone had *loosened* the bolts connecting the seat to the presidential carriage the night before!

DINK!

While he sat at Mary's bedside, Abe learned of two Union *victories* in unimaginably bloody battles.

MR. PRESIDENT! *GRANT* HAS TAKEN VICKSBURG AND *LEE* HAS BEEN BEATEN BACK AT GETTYSBURG!

General *Ulysses S. Grant* captured the port of Vicksburg, securing Union control of the Mississippi River and splitting the Confederacy in *two*. Scott's Anaconda Plan was succeeding!

Grant had been one of the most *successful* commanders on the Union side, despite rumors he *drank* too much.

After Vicksburg, Lincoln joked that if they could find out what brand Grant was *drinking*...

McClellan

GRANT

...he would send it to *all* his generals.

The day before, in the tiny town of *Gettysburg*, Pennsylvania, Union forces turned back the Confederate force led by General Robert E. Lee. There were *heavy* losses on both sides – worse than at Antietam.

Less than a year ago, the rebels had been riding high, but these dual defeats were a *crushing blow*.

NOW LEAVING PENNSYLVANIA COME BACK SOON!

In October 1863, Lincoln signed a proclamation making Thanksgiving a national holiday. He wanted people to *give thanks* for all the Union's victories.

His proclamation declared that we would "set apart and observe *the last Thursday of November*" as a day of thanks for all one has.

THE TRADITION OF EATING *TURKEY* ON THAT DATE WENT BACK TO THE LEGENDARY FIRST THANKSGIVING BETWEEN NATIVE AMERICANS AND PILGRIMS.

UNFORTUNATELY! ≶GULP≶

Lincoln also started a *new* tradition, pardoning a turkey from the feast.

THIS I LIKE BETTER!

Perhaps Abe got this idea from Tad's pet turkey, who freely wandered the White House grounds.

TAD, WILL YOUR BIRD VOTE FOR ME IN THE COMING ELECTION?

NO, PA — HE'S NOT OF AGE!

BALLOT

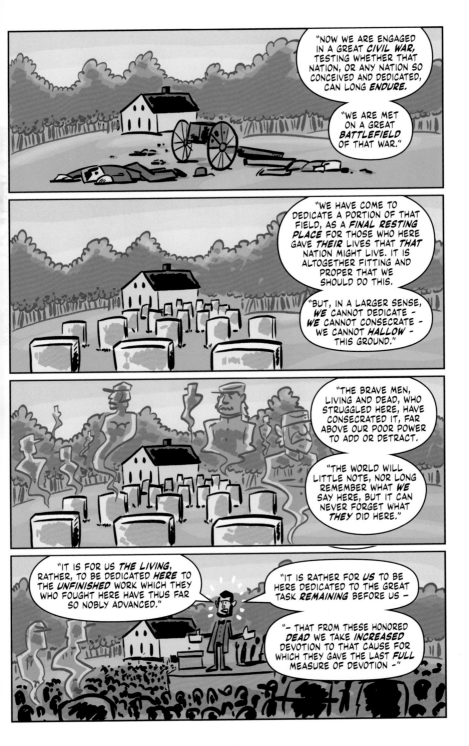

Because it made clear the Civil War was not really being fought over slavery, or states' rights, or any other specific issue but over the very idea of America herself:

It's the same reason George Washington was ready to ride out against the Whiskey Rebels during *his* presidency.

For thousands of years it was believed people were too stupid and scared to be ruled over by anything other than a small group of nobles and kings, by force.

Democracy is rule by the people — for the people — but by the laws that the people *themselves* create.

If some people can *ignore* those laws whenever they feel like it — then what's the good of making them in the first place?

That's just proof that people can't rule themselves!

The Gettysburg Address says that the *hope* that the US provided to the world, that people could decide *their own* future, was too important to let go without a fight.

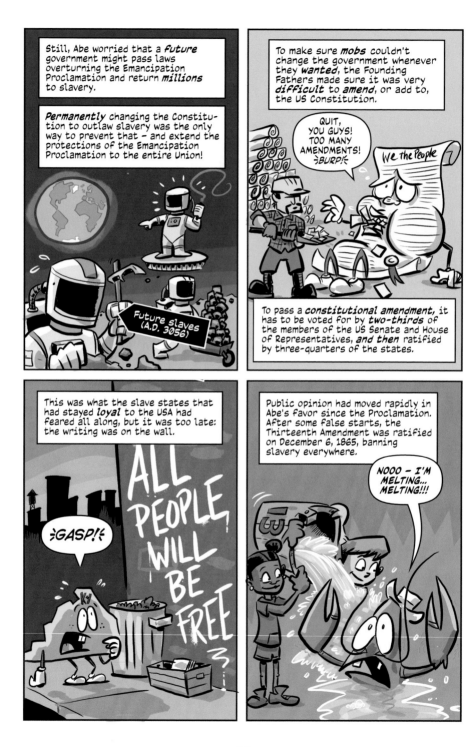

Still, Abe worried that a *future* government might pass laws overturning the Emancipation Proclamation and return *millions* to slavery.

Permanently changing the Constitution to outlaw slavery was the only way to prevent that – and extend the protections of the Emancipation Proclamation to the entire Union!

Future slaves (A.D. 3056)

To make sure *mobs* couldn't change the government whenever they *wanted*, the Founding Fathers made sure it was very *difficult* to *amend*, or add to, the US Constitution.

QUIT, YOU GUYS! TOO MANY AMENDMENTS! ₹BURP!₹

We the People

To pass a *constitutional amendment*, it has to be voted for by *two-thirds* of the members of the US Senate and House of Representatives, *and then* ratified by three-quarters of the states.

This was what the slave states that had stayed *loyal* to the USA had feared all along, but it was too late: the writing was on the wall.

₹GASP!₹

ALL PEOPLE WILL BE FREE

Public opinion had moved rapidly in Abe's favor since the Proclamation. After some false starts, the Thirteenth Amendment was ratified on December 6, 1865, banning slavery everywhere.

NOOO – I'M MELTING... MELTING!!!

Completely fed up with George McClellan's *bad attitude* and stop-and-start battlefield tactics, Abe had made *Ulysses S. Grant*, the hero of Vicksburg, the head of the Union army on March 8, 1864.

BOOT!

Congress brought back the rank of *lieutenant general*, not held by anyone since *George Washington*, to give to Grant as a sign of their faith in him.

GO GET 'EM, "U. S."!

The "Anaconda" continued to constrict around the Confederacy. Grant's army chased Lee's throughout Virginia. Abe and Mary could watch some of the fighting from the White House roof.

Once, when an army surgeon standing next to him got shot, Abe kept on watching the battle until a captain had to yell at him:

UGH!

"GET DOWN, YOU FOOL!"

The Election of 1864

Abe was up for reelection, and his Democratic Party opponent that year was none other than his former *top general*, the Young Napoleon *himself*, George McClellan.

ENOUGH OF THIS HORRIBLE WAR! IF ELECTED, I PROMISE TO END IT IMMEDIATELY!

UH... BUT WASN'T THAT YOUR JOB AS **GENERAL**?

"Stump speech" (get it)

YES, BUT I WAS **FIRED!**

YOU'RE **REALLY** LUCKY I'M NOT OLD ENOUGH TO **VOTE.**

Abe easily won the **Republican** nomination, recalling the story of a Dutch farmer:

"IT'S NOT BEST TO **SWAP HORSES** WHEN CROSSING STREAMS!"

Enough American voters were sick of fighting that McClellan's prospects looked *pretty good,* early on.

But then, on September 1, Union General Tecumseh Sherman captured the second-largest city in the Confederacy, *Atlanta*, Georgia, and Little Mac's prospects sank.

Unlike last time, Abe was elected in a stunning *landslide.* (Of course, also unlike last time, no Confederate states actually voted.)

PRIVATE! FETCH MY HORSE! WE'RE **OUTNUMBERED...** UGH!

Adding insult to injury, eighty percent of *soldiers* voted for Lincoln, *not* the ex-general!

Lincoln's **second** Inauguration Day was March 4, 1865. It was a grim, overcast day as crowds gathered at the Capitol...

...but as soon as Abe stepped forward to give his speech, the dark clouds parted and the sun began to shine.

"WITH MALICE TOWARD **NONE**; WITH CHARITY FOR **ALL**; WITH FIRMNESS IN THE **RIGHT**, AS GOD GIVES US TO **SEE** THE RIGHT...

"...LET US STRIVE ON TO FINISH THE WORK WE ARE IN; TO BIND UP THE NATION'S **WOUNDS**; TO CARE FOR HIM WHO SHALL HAVE BORNE THE BATTLE, AND FOR HIS WIDOW, AND FOR HIS ORPHAN –"

Abe was so popular that gamblers were **already** betting that he would win a **third** term in 1868...

"– TO DO ALL WHICH MAY ACHIEVE AND CHERISH A JUST AND A LASTING PEACE, AMONG OURSELVES, AND WITH **ALL** NATIONS."

...but they didn't know someone **else** was watching the speech with quite a bit of **malice!**

Richmond, Virginia, the Confederate capital, fell to Federal troops on April 3, 1865.

Abe and Tad toured the destroyed city not long thereafter.

The president soon found himself surrounded by a small team of black laborers.

"BLESS THE LORD!"

"HERE IS THE GREAT MESSIAH!"

Many fell to their knees. Embarrassed but deeply *moved* at the same time, Abe said:

"DO NOT KNEEL TO ME. THAT IS NOT RIGHT. YOU MUST KNEEL TO *GOD* ONLY, AND THANK HIM FOR THE LIBERTY YOU WILL HEREAFTER JOY."

The streets, observers said, became "suddenly alive" with jubilant African Americans.

The crowd followed Abe, Tad, and the sailors who protected them through the streets.

In two miles they reached the mansion that served as the Confederate White House.

HEY, PA, HOW COME THEIR PRESIDENT HOUSE LOOKS *BIGGER* THAN OUR PRESIDENT HOUSE – IT'S GOT *THREE* STORIES!

THE BIGGER THEY ARE THE HARDER THEY FALL, I GUESS....

You can still see it today – turn to "Places to Visit"!

President Davis and most of the CSA government had fled the city, so Tad and his dad toured an empty house.

"THIS MUST HAVE BEEN JEFFERSON DAVIS'S DESK."

He asked for a glass of water from the Union general then in charge of Richmond.

HOW SHOULD WE TREAT THE PEOPLE OF THE CITY WHO STAYED BEHIND, SIR?

OH ... "IF I WERE IN YOUR PLACE, I'D LET 'EM UP EASY.

"LET 'EM UP *EASY*."

101

Less than a week after Richmond fell, General Lee surrendered to Grant at a courthouse in nearby Appomattox, Virginia.

When Lincoln received the news, a great peace washed over *him*, too.

SINCE THE DAY I WALKED INTO THIS OFFICE AND GOT NOTICE OF FORT SUMTER, I'VE BEEN A *WARTIME PRESIDENT* – UNTIL *NOW!*

As the people of Washington, DC, heard news of victory, happy crowds gathered at the White House.

Candles were lit around the building at night to celebrate. Lincoln addressed the crowd, talking about what would come next.

AS I SAID IN MY INAUGURAL, I BELIEVE WE SHOULD WELCOME OUR SOUTHERN FRIENDS BACK WITH OPEN ARMS!

AS FOR THE FORMER SLAVES, THOSE WHO FOUGHT FOR THE UNION SHOULD BE GIVEN THE RIGHT TO *VOTE* – *IF* THEY CAN READ AND WRITE.

Though those proposals may sound pretty *mild* to us today, they greatly *angered* at least one man in the crowd.

On the night of April 14, 1865 – *Good Friday* – the Lincoln family split up to see two different performances in downtown DC.

Abe and Mary went to Ford's Theatre to see a comedy called *Our American Cousin.*

Abe's bodyguard had the night off and told the president he shouldn't go, but:

"IT HAS BEEN ADVERTISED THAT WE WILL BE THERE, AND I CANNOT DISAPPOINT THE PEOPLE."

Hey, what's this bill Abe is signing into law?

Tad, meanwhile, headed to Grover's Theatre to see a production of *Aladdin, or His Wonderful Lamp.* He had just turned twelve years old.

Thirty minutes in, a theater employee interrupted the performance:

I'M SORRY TO REPORT... THE PRESIDENT HAS BEEN SHOT!

The stunned silence at *Aladdin* was broken by Tad's cries:

THEY'VE KILLED HIM! THEY'VE KILLED HIM!

John Wilkes Booth knew that Lincoln was going to be at Ford's too, used his celebrity to slip unquestioned into the president's box, and shot Lincoln in the head.

His fellow conspirators tried to kill other members of the government, too.

Lewis Powell, who was with Booth at the White House, tried to stab Secretary of State Seward to death as he lay in bed, but he was fought off by Seward's family.

Another Booth assassin was supposed to kill Vice President Andrew Johnson while he slept in the hotel room directly beneath him, but he got cold feet and fled into the night.

Abe was brought to a home across the street from the theater, where doctors tried to save his life, but he died of his wounds by the next morning.

"NOW HE BELONGS TO THE AGES..."

Secretary of War Edwin Stanton

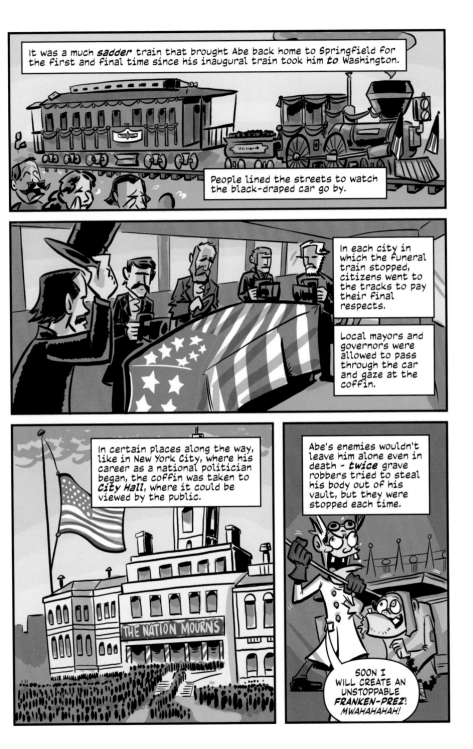

It was a much *sadder* train that brought Abe back home to Springfield for the first and final time since his inaugural train took him *to* Washington.

People lined the streets to watch the black-draped car go by.

In each city in which the funeral train stopped, citizens went to the tracks to pay their final respects.

Local mayors and governors were allowed to pass through the car and gaze at the coffin.

In certain places along the way, like in New York City, where his career as a national politician began, the coffin was taken to *City Hall*, where it could be viewed by the public.

THE NATION MOURNS

Abe's enemies wouldn't leave him alone even in death - *twice* grave robbers tried to steal his body out of his vault, but they were stopped each time.

SOON I WILL CREATE AN UNSTOPPABLE *FRANKEN-PREZ*! MWAHAHAHAH!

Incredibly, on the day he was shot, April 14, Lincoln signed a bill that wound up giving *future* presidents the protection they needed –

– that's right, just *hours* before he was murdered, Abe signed the bill that created the *United States Secret Service!*

Originally, the Secret Service was created to go after crooks who *counterfeited* US currency (which is why it's part of the Treasury Department).

FREEZE, MONOPOLY BOY!

In fact, it would take the assassinations of *two more presidents* – James Garfield in 1881 –

MY WORK IS *DONE* HERE!

BANG!

– and William McKinley in 1901 –

HIS MONEY IS REAL! HE'S CLEAN!

POW!

– before Congress decided to make the Secret Service *also* serve as the bodyguards to the president.

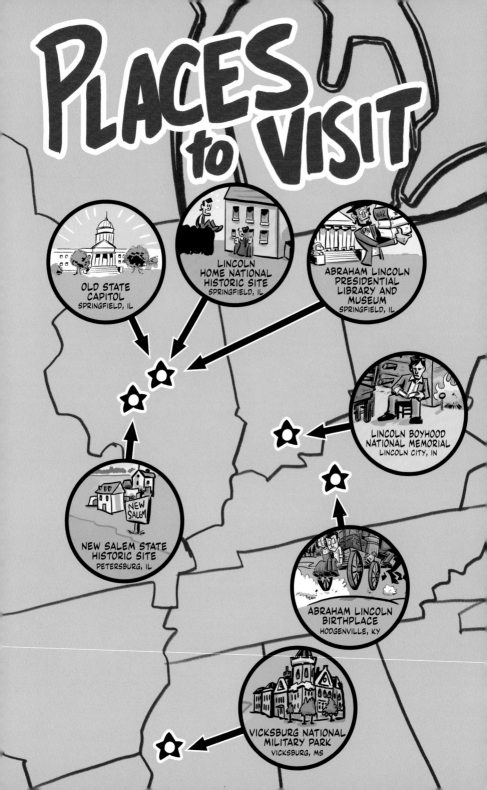

BIBLIOGRAPHY

Brookhiser, Richard. *Founders' Son: A Life of Abraham Lincoln.* New York: Basic Books, 2014. Lincoln's life as seen through his influences, from Founding Fathers like George Washington to the Holy Bible.

Dirck, Brian R. *Lincoln and the Constitution.* Carbondale, IL: Southern Illinois University Press, 2012. A very short but helpful look at Lincoln's legal mind, both as a practicing attorney and as president.

Eighmey, Rae Katherine. *Abraham Lincoln in the Kitchen: A Culinary View of Lincoln's Life and Times.* Washington, DC: Smithsonian Books, 2013. A super-fun journey of the author through Lincoln's life by the food he ate and prepared at each stage of the way, filled with recipes you can do yourself!

Goodwin, Doris Kearns. *Team of Rivals: The Political Genius of Abraham Lincoln.* New York: Simon & Schuster, 2005. A classic that is not just a biography of Abe but all his major cabinet members too.

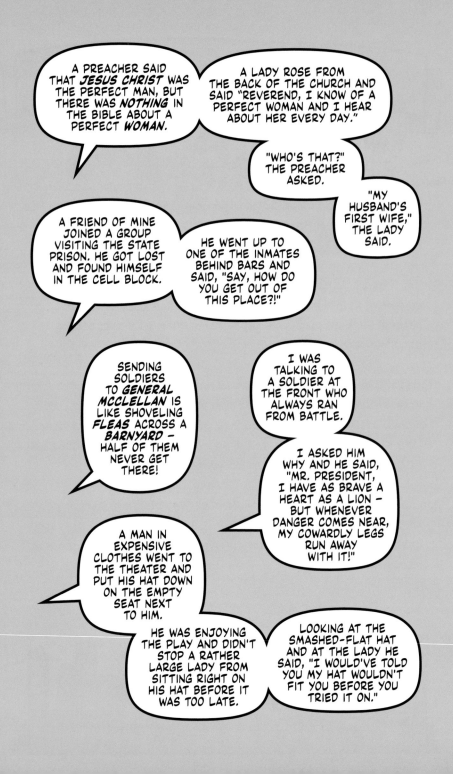

IMPEACH (v): to charge a member of the government with misconduct

INAUGURATION (n): a ceremony to mark the beginning of something (like, say, a presidency)

LEGISLATURE (n): the governing body of a country that votes bills into laws

MALICE (n): the desire to hurt or do evil

MEMORIAL (n): a statue or structure (or both) built to remind one of a person or event

MILITIA (n): a military force of civilians raised to help out a country's army in an emergency

MILL (n): a building that can grind wheat into flour

MIMIC (v): to imitate, usually for fun

PARAMOUNT (adj): the most important

PATENT (n): a government license giving an inventor sole rights to an invention

PAYMASTER (n): the officer who pays soldiers of an army

PENSION (n): a regular payment a retired person gets from his former employer

PLANTATION (n): a really big farm

PROPOSITION (n): a suggestion of a plan, usually in business

RELUCTANT (adj): "I don't really wanna"

RESOLUTION (n): a formal expression of opinion by a legislature

SOVEREIGNTY (n): the authority a state has to govern itself

TREATY (n): a formal agreement between two or more nation-states

ULTIMATE (adj): the best, or last, or both!

WIDOW (n): a wife whose husband has died

GLOSSARY

ABOLITION (n): getting rid of a practice or law, legally

ADVOCATE (n): someone who argues in favor of someone else

AMENDMENT (n): a change to the US Constitution (there are 27 as of this writing)

ANACONDA (n): a big snake native to South America

BILL (vs LAW) (n): a draft of a proposed law that has to be voted on before it can become law

CHORD (n): a group of musical notes played at the same time

CHRONICLE (n): a written account of history, in the order in which events happened

COMMEND (v): to give somebody a task (formally)

CONSECRATE (v): to declare something sacred or connected to God

COUNTERFEIT (n): fake

DANDY (n): a vain, usually wealthy man who cares a little too much about his appearance

DILEMMA (n): a difficult choice between equally good (or bad) options

DISRUPT (v): to change or destroy the nature of something

ELITE (n): a group of people in society seen as superior due to wealth or status

ENDURE (v): to remain in existence

FLATBOAT (n): a cargo boat with a flat bottom (as opposed to a curved hull) for use in shallow water, like in a river

HALLOWED (adj): what something is after it has been consecrated (see above)

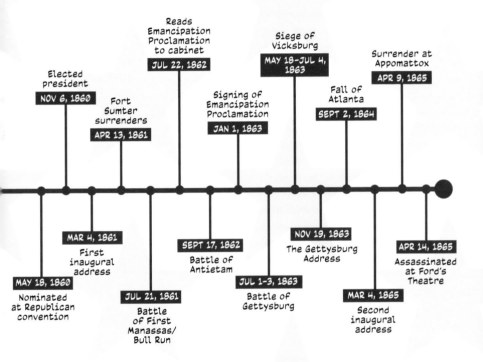

Elected president
NOV 6, 1860

Fort Sumter surrenders
APR 13, 1861

Reads Emancipation Proclamation to cabinet
JUL 22, 1862

Signing of Emancipation Proclamation
JAN 1, 1863

Siege of Vicksburg
MAY 18-JUL 4, 1863

Fall of Atlanta
SEPT 2, 1864

Surrender at Appomattox
APR 9, 1865

MAY 18, 1860
Nominated at Republican convention

MAR 4, 1861
First inaugural address

JUL 21, 1861
Battle of First Manassas/ Bull Run

SEPT 17, 1862
Battle of Antietam

JUL 1-3, 1863
Battle of Gettysburg

NOV 19, 1863
The Gettysburg Address

MAR 4, 1865
Second inaugural address

APR 14, 1865
Assassinated at Ford's Theatre

TIMELINE

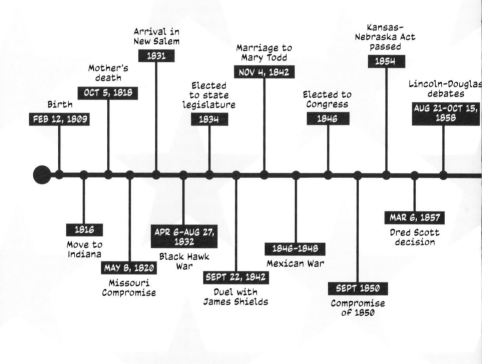

Birth
FEB 12, 1809

Mother's death
OCT 5, 1818

Arrival in New Salem
1831

Elected to state legislature
1834

Marriage to Mary Todd
NOV 4, 1842

Elected to Congress
1846

Kansas–Nebraska Act passed
1854

Lincoln–Douglas debates
AUG 21–OCT 15, 1858

1816
Move to Indiana

APR 6–AUG 27, 1832
Black Hawk War

1846–1848
Mexican War

MAR 6, 1857
Dred Scott decision

MAY 8, 1820
Missouri Compromise

SEPT 22, 1842
Duel with James Shields

SEPT 1850
Compromise of 1850

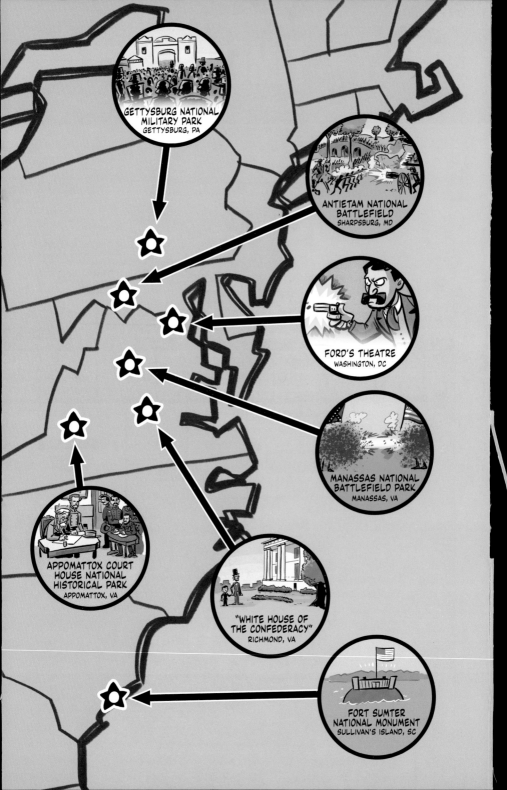

Leidner, Gordon. *Lincoln's Gift: How Humor Shaped Lincoln's Life and Legacy.* Naperville, IL: Cumberland House, 2015. A great biography telling all of Abe's many, many, many jokes, gags, quips, and funny stories.

Lincoln, Abraham. *The Poems of Abraham Lincoln.* Bedford, MA: Applewood Books, 1991. Abe used his pen to write verse from time to time, including "The Bear Hunt," a verse of which is in our book.

McPherson, James M. *Embattled Rebel: Jefferson Davis as Commander in Chief.*
New York: Penguin Books, 2014. There are two sides to every story, and this tells of the challenges the president of the Confederacy faced to win the war and beat Lincoln.

Stashower, Daniel. *The Hour of Peril: The Secret Plot to Murder Lincoln Before the Civil War.* New York: Minotaur Books, 2013. As exciting as any fictional thriller, this tells of the Pinkerton detectives' endeavors to thwart the attempt in Baltimore to stop his inauguration train.

Wead, Doug. *All the Presidents' Children: Triumph and Tragedy in the Lives of America's First Families.* New York: Atria Books, 2003. A great book full of interesting stories about all presidential kids, particularly Tad's and Willie's antics.

White, Ronald C., Jr. *The Eloquent President: A Portrait of Lincoln Through His Words.* New York: Random House, 2005. Abe was probably our best writer president, and this looks at how he composed his greatest speeches, from the Gettysburg Address on down.